A No-Good Dog

Written by John Lockyer
Illustrated by Trevor Pye

Sundance was Danny's dog. He got her from the dog pound.
On the way home, Sundance sat on the seat between Danny
and his father.

"Sundance isn't just a pet," Danny's dad told him.
"She'll have to work for her dinner like the other farm dogs."

Sundance blinked at Danny's dad, then got sick over his pants.
It was not a good start.

A few days later, Dad said, "Sundance can be our guard dog."

But, when visitors arrived, Sundance ran into the yard
to meet them. She only sniffed and licked their hands.
She never barked. Danny's dad said Sundance was
a no-good guard dog.

Then Dad said, "Sundance can be a sheep dog." But Sundance just chased the sheep everywhere. She didn't listen to Dad calling her. "Sundance is a no-good sheep dog," said Dad.

And now Sundance was in trouble again. She had pulled plants out of the garden. "Look what Sundance has done," growled Dad. "Something's got to be done about her."

Danny wasn't sure what his father meant, but he knew he'd find out soon enough.

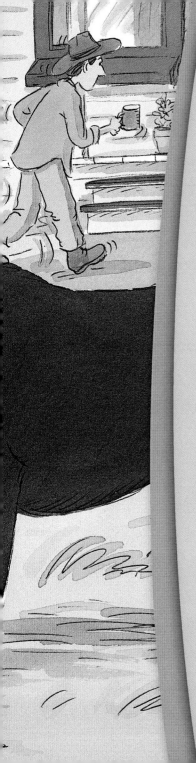

Later that day, Dad said to Danny, "I told Matt Jennings that Sundance is no good, but he still wants her."

Matt Jennings owned the farm across the road. "What does he want her for?" asked Danny.

"A house dog," said his dad.

"No!" shouted Danny. **"Sundance is mine!"**

"She licks strangers and barks at birds," said his dad. "She digs up the garden. She brings dead rats inside, but won't bring in the sheep. This farm makes just enough to feed us. We can't afford her."

Danny ran across the yard and slumped down against the woodshed wall. A rough tongue began to lick his ear. Danny knew that if he looked at Sundance he would cry.

Danny nagged his father for days about Sundance. "I'll train her. Please let me keep her."

His dad just shook his head. "She's no good. She's going." But Danny didn't give up.

One day, Danny's dad said, "We'll forget the jobs for today. Let's take Sundance to the hills."

Danny grinned. "You mean I can keep her?"

His dad turned away. "Matt will be here at dinnertime. We'll have to be back by then."

Danny felt happier than he had for a long time. His father hadn't said no.

Danny, his father and Sundance made their way up the hill track. Suddenly, Sundance barked. A rabbit darted away into the trees and Sundance ran after it. Danny followed.

"Don't go too far," his father called.

Danny could see Sundance's wagging tail up the hill. He climbed after her, but, when he reached the top, Sundance was gone.

Danny followed the track, whistling and calling. He saw Sundance crouched on a flat rock in the middle of a rockslide. Danny frowned. Rockslides were dangerous. He knew that, if anything heavy landed on it, the slide would start moving.

"Sundance!" he called.

Sundance whined, but didn't move, and Danny knew that he would have to go to her.

He'd crossed rockslides before. He knew he had to run fast and light.

Danny dashed onto the rocks. He lifted his knees high and pulled his feet free of the shifting stones.

Danny reached the rock and grabbed Sundance's collar. But Sundance jumped and knocked him off balance. They both began to slide.

Danny let Sundance go and she ran to safety. He tried to follow, but the rocks began to shift downwards . . .

faster . . .

and faster . . .

Soon the rocks were above Danny's waist. He tried to throw off his backpack, but it got twisted around his chest.

He thrashed his arms around, trying to stay upright, but the rocks were swallowing him. He screamed, then disappeared under the rocks.

Danny's dad heard Sundance barking. He looked up the trail and saw Sundance. She barked again. Dad frowned. Something must be wrong.

Sundance turned and ran back up the track with Dad close behind. They climbed the hill. Dad could see Danny's red cap lying on the rocks.

Dad ran down onto the rocks as lightly as he could. Most of the rocks had shifted downhill now. They weren't moving any more. When he reached Danny's cap, he began to scrape away the stones. "Come on, Sundance!" he said. "Help me dig."

But Sundance ran down to a rocky hump. She barked and began to dig. Dad ran to the hump and began to dig, too.

Dad's fingers touched Danny's backpack! He slid his hands under Danny's shoulders and dragged him free. Danny had crossed his arms over his face, and he only had some grazes and a bump on the head.

"Are you OK?" asked Dad.

Danny sat up. "Yes," he said as he patted Sundance.

"Sundance saved you," said his dad. "She showed me where to dig."

When they got home, Matt Jennings was waiting for them. "Is that the no-good dog you're giving away?" he asked.

"No," said Dad. "That's Sundance. She's a do-good dog. We'd never give her away!"

A No-Good Dog is a **Narrative**.

A **narrative** has an introduction. It tells . . .

- **who** the story is about (the characters)
- **where** the story happened
- **when** the story happened.

Introduction	
Who	
Where	
When	When Danny got Sundance from the pound.

A narrative has a **problem** and a **solution**.

Problem

Solution

▬▬ Guide Notes

Title: A No-Good Dog
Stage: Fluency

Text Form: Narrative
Approach: Guided Reading
Processes: Thinking Critically, Exploring Language, Processing Information
Written and Visual Focus: Illustrative Text

THINKING CRITICALLY
(sample questions)
- What do you think this story could be about? Look at the title and discuss.
- Look at the cover. What do you think a *No-Good Dog* is?
- Look at pages 2 and 3. What do you think *She'll have to work for her dinner* means?
- Look at pages 4 and 5. Why do you think Sundance pulled the plants out of the garden?
- Look at pages 6 and 7. Do you think Dad is being fair? Why or why not?
- Look at pages 8 and 9. Why do you think Dad turned away when Danny asked if he could keep Sundance?
- Look at pages 10 and 11. Do you think Danny should have followed Sundance? Why or why not?
- Look at pages 12 and 13. Why do you think Danny tried to throw off his backpack?
- Look at pages 14 and 15. How do you know Dad was worried?

EXPLORING LANGUAGE

Terminology
Spread, author and illustrator credits, imprint information, ISBN number

Vocabulary
Clarify: do-good, thrashed, rockslide, nagged, whined, dashed
Adjectives: *dead* rats, *rough* tongue, *wagging* tail, *flat* rock
Pronouns: they, he, she, me, her, it
Focus the students' attention on **homonyms**, **antonyms** and **synonyms** if appropriate.